WORLDBUILDING:
FROM SMALL TOWNS TO ENTIRE UNIVERSES

To Ray —

WORLDBUILDING:
FROM SMALL TOWNS TO ENTIRE UNIVERSES

Build those, worlds.

New York Times Bestselling Author
KEVIN J. ANDERSON

WordFire Press
Colorado Springs, Colorado

WORLDBUILDING:
FROM SMALL TOWNS TO ENTIRE UNIVERSES
THE MILLION DOLLAR WRITING SERIES
Copyright © 2015 WordFire, Inc.

The authors and publisher have strived to be as accurate and complete as possible in creating the Million Dollar Writing series. We don't believe in magical outcomes from our advice. We do believe in hard work and helping others. The advice in our Million Dollar Writing series is intended to offer new tools and approaches to writing. We make no guarantees about any individual's ability to get results or earn money with our ideas, information, tools or strategies. We do want to help by giving great content, direction and strategies to move writers forward faster. Nothing in this book is a promise or guarantee of future book sales or earnings. Any numbers referenced in this series are estimates or projections, and should not be considered exact, actual or as a promise of potential earnings. All numbers are for the purpose of illustration. The sole purpose of these materials is to educate and entertain. Any perceived slights to specific organizations or individuals are unintentional. The publisher and authors are not engaged in rendering legal, accounting, financial, or other professional services. If legal or expert assistance is required, the services of a competent professional should be sought.

ISBN: 978-1-61475-375-9

Cover design by Janet McDonald

Art Director Kevin J. Anderson

Cover artwork images by Dollar Photo Club

Book Design by RuneWright, LLC
www.RuneWright.com

Published by
WordFire Press, an imprint of
WordFire, Inc.
PO Box 1840
Monument CO 80132

Kevin J. Anderson & Rebecca Moesta, Publishers

WordFire Press Trade Paperback Edition October 2015
Printed in the USA
wordfirepress.com

CONTENTS

ONE:
CREATING UNIVERSES, BIG AND SMALL

I've written 130 novels, and I've built a lot of worlds—some of them entirely from scratch, others similar to the neighborhoods I can visit every day, with just simple modifications and altered details. I like to paint on a big literary canvas, and I like to fill in all the details.

In my space opera series, the Saga of Seven Suns and the Saga of Shadows, I created the vast Spiral Arm, with rival galactic empires,

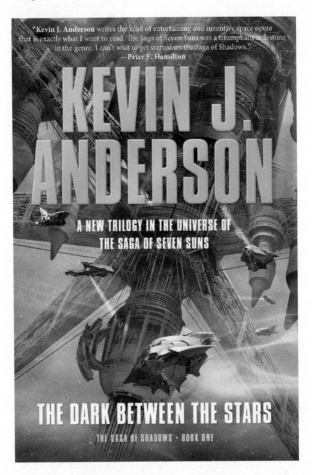

trading conglomerates, diverse cultures (human and non-human), hundreds of planets, exotic climates, bizarre alien races, and extraterrestrial life forms—all as a backdrop for my characters to let me tell their stories.

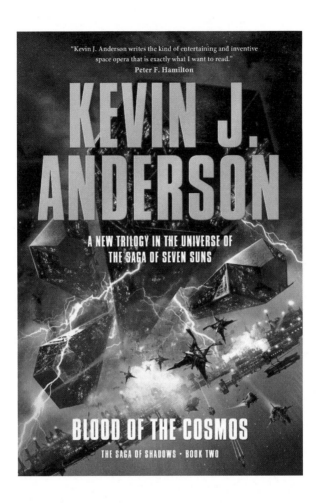

In my Dan Shamble, Zombie P.I. series, I took a more whimsical fantastic approach on a modern-day America ten years after an utterly improbable sequence of cosmic coincidences unleashed werewolves, ghosts, vampires, mummies, and zombies back into the world. The monsters have set up a section of the city, the Unnatural Quarter, where they can live and

let live (so to speak). They operate embalming parlors, cafes, gambling joints, All Day/All Nite fitness centers (including treadmills without mirrors, so as not to embarrass the vampire clientele). And, yes, zombie detective agencies.

The monsters experience the same types of problems that normal people do, though maybe a bit more extreme. It's all played for laughs,

and it may seem silly—but I mapped out the rules, laid down the details and followed them consistently throughout.

In my ambitious "sailing ships and sea monsters" nautical fantasy trilogy, Terra

Incognita, I developed a world much like Medieval Europe during the Crusades, with a partially unmapped world, ambitious sailing expeditions—as well as a smattering of magic, and of course sea monsters. Even though the fictional world was closely based on the Portugal of Prince Henry the Navigator or the Mediterranean of the Crusades, I still had to understand basic questions such as: How do sailing ships work? How do the sailors navigate? Does this civilization have accurate clocks (vital for navigation)? Do the navies have gunpowder? Do the countries have the printing press? In Uraba, my continent modeled after desert-like Arabia, where did they get the trees to build their wooden ships? Where are the mines for the metals they needed?

All those questions had to be answered—and the answers in turn drove and shaped the storyline.

I have done a lot of work in established universes based on films, TV, or well-known novels. Often the audiences are already extremely familiar with the characters and details. For instance, I've written numerous projects in the universes of Star Wars, Dune, X-Files, Batman, Superman, Star Trek, and most recently in the Heroes Reborn TV show. When I worked on Star Wars, I had access to multiple reference books, information gathered by generations of fans and Lucasfilm experts. In my Superman novel, *The Last Days of Krypton*, I had to pull together almost ninety years of scattered hints and assertions about Superman's home planet, about his father Jor-El, about how Krypton had exploded ... and much of the established canon was completely contradictory. I had to find some way to synthesize it, force it all to make sense. And sometimes such challenges led to quite wonderful solutions.

When my friend Neil Peart, the drummer and lyricist for the legendary rock group Rush, invited me to work with him on a storyline and novel for their steampunk fantasy concept album "Clockwork Angels," he told me his vision for a pleasant Victorian-era world run by a rigid but benevolent figure named the Watchmaker. In Albion, alchemy works, and the Watchmaker had discovered the secret of creating not only gold, but also a plentiful alchemical energy source called coldfire. Albion was wealthy (because of all that gold) and comfortable (because of all that cheap energy), practically a utopia. The Watchmaker wasn't a brutal dictator; he just wanted everything to run efficiently.

But of course, not everyone wants that. Enter his nemesis, the Anarchist—a "freedom extremist" who wants to destroy all vestiges of order and civilization, so human beings can achieve true freedom by solving all of their own problems. But not everyone likes chaos either. Our hero, Owen Hardy, is a young man caught between the two forces.

When I started asking Neil detailed questions about the steampunk world of Albion, he said, "You're the master worldbuilder. I want to see what you come up with." So I started thinking … if gold was so plentiful, how would the economy work? Would silver then be more valued, as a rarer metal? Could people travel about freely? From the story, there had to be airships, pirates, lost cities, a steampunk carnival.

Neil made it clear that he did not want Albion to be a harsh dystopia, but a relatively pleasant place. Most people really do want the trains to run on time, and they want to be confident of a nice home, a comfortable life, and food for the table. Not everyone would be comfortable with too-rigid laws, however, so there were outliers, people who pushed the rules … like a traveling steampunk carnival or a hearty airship captain.

I began to sketch out the network of Albion's small towns, the steamliner routes, a

traveling airborne train whose mournful whistle would inspire dreams in a small-town boy like Owen Hardy. Eventually, I fleshed out the world so beautifully and added so many details, which sparked so many ideas for countless other stories and characters, we couldn't fit it all into one book, and so we wrote a companion novel, *Clockwork Lives*.

●　　●　　●

In this book, I'll lay out some of my worldbuilding techniques, show you some of the puzzle pieces you'll need to fit together, the blanks you'll have to fill in.

Building a world depends on more than just drawing a map and imagining some terrain. A fully fleshed-out fictional world has cultures and economics, varying climates, religions, arts, politics, social expectations. After I've guided you through all of the considerations, you'll be ready to build your own fictional world.

But you don't have to stop at just one.

Two:
Everyday
Worldbuilding

Even the most exotic fictional worlds are built from everyday details. Let me tell you about the small town where I grew up. I'll paint a picture with words and details.

I spent my childhood in the tiny southern Wisconsin town of Franksville, population 250. It was a place of farms, country roads, neighbors who didn't lock their doors, bicycles, cornfields, and treehouses … and not at all a place for a nerdy kid who liked to read comics.

It was a cross between Norman Rockwell and Norman Bates.

The entire vicinity around Franksville, Wisconsin, was centered on one industry—the sauerkraut factory, home of Frank's sauerkraut in pretty green cans that were shipped out nationwide (or worldwide, for all I knew). All the farmers for miles around grew fields of

cabbages. As a little kid I would watch trucks overloaded with cabbage heads rolling down the county highway. Every once in a while, one would fall off, and we kids would grab it and bring our prize home … even though none of us much cared for raw cabbage.

The sauerkraut factory processed the cabbage, fermented it, and then canned it. All the waste cabbage water and undesirable sauerkraut was dumped into drainage ditches. Now, the sauerkraut factory make kraut all year long, and in Wisconsin we have cold winters—so, all the rotten sauerkraut juice dumped into the drainage ditches would freeze solid. My mom told me about when she was a girl how she and her friends would go ice skating on the frozen sauerkraut juice pond. (She also says they learned very quickly not to slip and fall down.)

Then spring would arrive, along with warmer weather. The frozen kraut juice would thaw … and then it would *rot*, and an incredible stench would waft up from the environs of the factory. Our house was downwind, so we got the full brunt of it.

And now, as I mentioned in the introduction, I'm writing a series about a *zombie* character. Cause and effect? You decide.

Every summer, Franksville would held the Kraut Festival, with midway rides and games, crowds from all over southern Wisconsin. My mom was actually the sauerkraut queen of 1957 (I've seen the photos). One of the main events at the Franksville Kraut Festival was the "international championship sauerkraut eating contest." Contestants from as far away as Germany and Japan would join local champions, all of them seated at a table on the big stage as the crowds gathered. Then each contestant received a plate piled high with a full pound of steaming kraut—and when the buzzer sounded, they had 30 seconds to down it all. After a frenzy of activity, the winner would grasp his trophy, hold it up to applause, then bolt behind the stage to vomit out all that rapidly swallowed sauerkraut.

(I know this because my friends and I once sneaked behind the stage to watch, and we witnessed the entire spectacle.)

●   ●   ●

So why did I tell you all that? I was building you a world—the world of Franksville, Wisconsin ... just a small town that some would consider ordinary, but I hope I've given you a colorful enough picture so you can see what makes that place unique.

You probably believed everything in my description (I assure you it's all true). Why did you believe? Because of all the little details. Anybody can paint with broad, general strokes and tell basic things about a fictional world, but when you include details like ice skating on a frozen sauerkraut juice pond, or the cabbage heads falling off the trucks, or the kraut-eating contest and its stomach churning end ... nobody would know to make up those things, unless she had actually been there and experienced it.

To create a believable world, whether it's a small town in Wisconsin or a giant galactic empire, paint your picture with broad strokes, give your reader the background information necessary, *but also add the little details*, tiny points of veracity that your audience can *see* and *believe in*.

On my last visit to Australia, I spent time talking with my fellow author Bevan McGuinness. Bevan has done a lot of hiking in the Outback, and since I'm an avid hiker from Colorado, we exchanged hiking stories. He told me about a particularly nasty obstacle that hikers frequently encountered in the bush. The vicious flowering grass called spinifex. The flower heads are like thistles when they bloom, big, fluffy, and white, looking like tempting

cotton balls. Fields of spinifex often cover the trails, ready to trap unwary hikers. But even though the spinifex looks fluffy and cottony, it's filled with thin, sharp spines, and as you walk through the field of spinifex, the large flowers pierce and poke and stick to everything.

Bevan says that he can always spot amateur and unprepared hikers by the ones who wear long pants instead of shorts when pushing through a spinifex obstruction. That surprised me. "Don't you want protection from the thorns," I asked.

He explained that, yes, with bare legs you get poked and scratched by the spines—but that's all. You take your wounds and move on. But for anyone wearing long pants, all those spines poke through the fabric, then break off and remain stuck there ... so that all day long the needles constantly scratch and tear at the skin. At night around the campfire, seasoned hikers would pluck a few leftover spinifex thorns out of their skin and dress the scratches. The amateur hikers, though, would have to take off their pants, turn them inside out, and spend hours extracting out one spinifex spine at a time ... and then also bandage their far more numerous scratches and cuts.

A little detail, but a real one. Not something you can make up ... unless you've actually been there and seen it. A *real* detail for worldbuilding.

THREE:
QUESTIONS ARE YOUR BEST BUILDING BLOCKS

So, you want quick answers? Not so fast.

Questions often spark more imagination and more ideas than straightforward answers do. Therefore, ask a lot of questions, keep track of your answers, then ask more questions to build on the previous answers.

Suppose I gave you a simple challenge to describe something you're all familiar with? Say, for example we ask you to describe ... Earth. Scientists, writers, artists, psychologists ... in fact everybody *on Earth* has tried to describe the world in one way or another. As an inhabitant of Earth, you've spent your entire life picking up details, learning about the natives, the culture, the economy, the geography, the history, and so on.

How would you describe "Earth" as a setting for your story? What details would you choose to focus on?

Fortunately, creating a world for a novel or a short story doesn't need to be quite so rigorous, but you do need to *convey* a sense of a lot more details and a lot more growth without necessarily including every tiny nuance.

You, the writer, can make up just about anything you like—then build on it, so long as it's internally consistent. If you're writing a fantasy adventure, do you have a magic system developed? Do you know the rules as to when magic works and when it doesn't—and what it costs? A powerful wizard character can't be just a surprise grab box of magic miracles; he can't just pull out a charmed amulet with a "spell of plot convenience." You have to know all these details so the reader can buy into your world.

Ask your questions, then align your answers with all the other answers and details you've developed from the first round of questions. Then go back and ask more questions. Most important, play the most ruthless, geekiest fanboy skeptic: with every answer, ask, *Does it make sense?*

But we can't have you just asking random questions. For any good universe-creator, the answers need to build on one another and spark deeper, richer world creation.

For that, we'll start with an ingredients list.

FOUR:
A
WORLDBUILDING
INGREDIENTS
LIST

When I was a college student and aspiring writer, I got involved in role-playing games and in small press magazines. There, I built a circle of friends who were also aspiring writers with similar goals. One of these authors was Michael A. Stackpole, who had formed his own gaming company, Flying Buffalo, that produced role-playing game modules, each one called a MythosPak.

Each MythosPak was basically a ready-built world for RPG'ers to play in; a rich setting for their game. At the time I was 18, Mike was 23. He hired me to do one of his MythosPaks, even paid me a few hundred dollars for it (which at the time was one of the biggest writing checks I had ever received). His guidelines were very detailed, and I worked through them to create a fantasy world that described all aspects of the culture, history, monetary system, religion, geography, etc. I had never asked all those questions before. It seemed never to end!

But I began writing, filling in the blanks, then filling in more blanks, then expanding on what I had already created, which led to a more detailed picture. It was like a flower unfolding, getting bigger and bigger and more detailed. I did so much work on that MythosPak that I used the world I created as the backdrop for my first three fantasy novels, The Gamearth Trilogy.

In doing that exercise, I learned a great deal on how much work goes into building an entire world. Although I've since lost those formal notes for the MythosPak, I remembered what I had done. I learned how to do worldbuilding by practice and by instinct.

Years later, when my stepson was in a fourth grade social studies class, his teacher used a technique to bring other lands and cultures to life for the students. He called it PERSIA. (I've since learned that this is a common technique in schools—and it's a pretty good one.)

PERSIA stands for: *Political, Economic, Religion, Society, Intellectual,* and *Arts.*

That's a very neat breakdown of categories and a good starting point. But as I worked with it and began to formalize all the steps I use in building a completely real and believable fictional world, I realized there were other vital ingredients missing. So I expanded the concept, reorganized it, and made it into a far less pronounceable acronym:

GCPESRIAH

Don't worry—it doesn't have to be pronounceable, it just has to be *useful*.

These are my key elements to consider and develop for a fully formed fictional world:

- Geography

- Climate

- Politics

- Economic

- Social

- Religion

- Intellectual/Science

- Arts

- History

4.1
GEOGRAPHY

If we're going to build a world, let's start with the *world itself*—the geography, the landscape. Are your characters in a giant desert like Frank Herbert's *Dune*? Is it an ice planet like Hoth from *The Empire Strikes Back*? Is it a lush landscape with forests and mountains like Middle Earth (or New Zealand, as Peter Jackson would have it)?

I've received a lot of manuscripts from aspiring fantasy authors. (No I don't have time to read them, and, no, please don't send me yours.) It seems that a requirement for any epic fantasy novel is a big map of the world, with suitably spaced hazards from west to east, so the characters can encounter sufficient adventures.

Some of the maps I've seen are simply ridiculous, drawn by writers with a great deal of story imagination, but not necessarily any geographical common sense. Oh, each map has the requisite frozen wastes in the north, impassable deserts in the south, oceans to the east and west.

Don't succumb to "wistful fictional geography."

I remember one map in particular, a fantasy land ringed by towering mountains on all sides—north, south, east and west. Rivers flowed from the mountains into the heartland. (Yes, rivers do tend to start in the mountains, but they drain *toward the sea*, not the middle of the land.) It was quite a remarkable world actually.

This particular map also had trackless and treacherous swamps pushing up against impenetrable sand-dune deserts, like the Louisiana bayous right next to the Sahara. Hmm, how would that occur? Cities had sprung up in rugged inhospitable places—for defense, I suppose, but without much consideration for trade. Historically speaking, settlements tend to arise where there's a *reason* for a lot of people to be: rivers or harbors, major crossroads, the site of important resources. There are usually reasons why humans put settlements where they do.

I remember a big budget fantasy movie, in which our heroes had to complete a difficult quest to steal a powerful talisman from the Big Baddy. The Big Baddy had built a sinister, evil-looking tower in a vast desert surrounded by cracked dirt, lava rock, and black slag—out in the middle of nowhere. There were no roads, no rivers … and yet the Big Baddy had filled the evil fortress with thousands of monster henchmen.

It made great cinema. It looked very scary. But … Huh? Who builds a gigantic population center and towering fortress in the middle of a wasteland? Where did the water come from? How was food delivered for all of the monster henchmen? Any villain should have thought of those things! How was the fortress constructed?

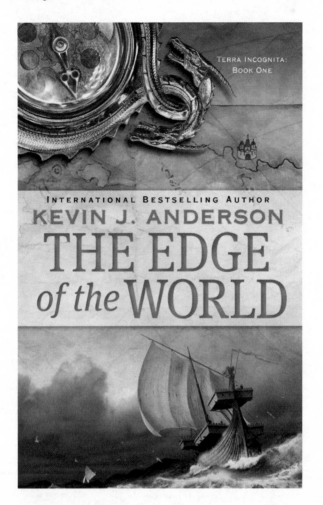

Where did the materials come from out in the wasteland, and how did all that stone and metal arrive if there were no roads? (Yes, you could postulate that the Big Baddy used a magic spell to construct the tower, but in most cases I would advise not to rely on Spontaneous Construction.)

In a properly created world, the geography itself can drive the story. As an example, let me walk you through the map for my Terra Incognita fantasy trilogy.

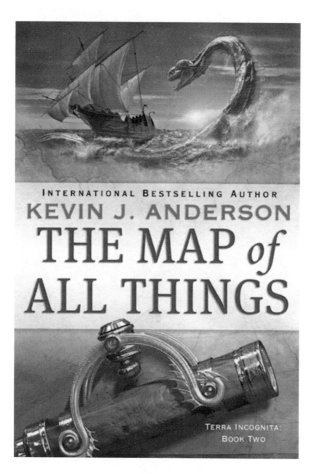

The basic idea comes from the Prester John legend that became popular during the Crusades, when an as yet undiscovered

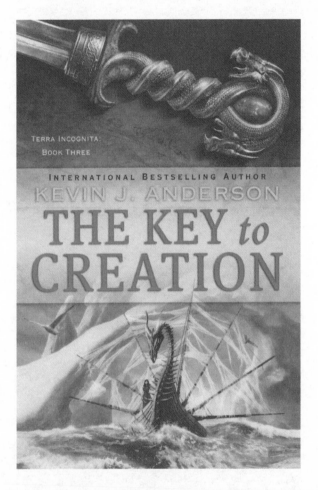

Christian kingdom was rumored to exist far beyond the horizon. This kingdom was ruled by Prester John, a man who possessed the actual

Holy Grail as well as the Fountain of Youth and increasing numbers of magical items as the legend grow over the years.

A very sketchy historical paraphrase: During the time, the Moors were sweeping through Northern Africa across the Straits of Gibraltar and invading Spain and greater Europe. Some desperate Christian rulers decided that if only they could find the lost kingdom of Prester John, he would be a powerful ally, who would bring his own armies to help Christian Europe drive the Muslims back. The search for Prester John was one of the reasons why so many of the influential historical voyages of discovery were launched—Vasco da Gama, Balboa, and others who sailed around uncharted Africa in search of a new continent. They did discover a whole new continent and eventually a passage around the Cape of Good Hope and up to India .... although they never did find Prester John.

I used that as the core idea for my Terra Incognita trilogy, in my own fantasy world with my own cultures and my own history. My world

has two continents—Tierra (the equivalent of Christian Europe) and Uraba (the equivalent of Muslim Arabia). The two continents are joined by a very narrow isthmus, at the center of which is the great city of Ishalem, an ancient city considered sacred to both religions (like Jerusalem).

After centuries of friction and occasional clashes, the king of Tierra finally reaches a peace accord with the Sultan of Uraba. They meet in the sacred city of Ishalem to sign their treaty, and there is much rejoicing. Unfortunately, during all that rejoicing, someone accidentally starts a fire, which gets out of control, and the entire holy city burns down. Both the Tierrans and the Urabans blame the other side, and the bloody war explodes....

Now, back to the geography: Because the two continents are connected by a narrow isthmus, the sacred city becomes a natural bottleneck. That geographical fact drives a great deal of trade and military strategy. Ships go up and down the outer coast, but they cannot get into the Middle Sea, a huge body of water like the Mediterranean on the other side of the isthmus. Therefore, many major roads and transport caravans take goods from the western side of the Isthmus to waiting ships on the other (until, much later in the trilogy, one of the leaders decides to dig a canal to connect the two bodies of water).

So how does all this tie in with the Prester John legend? In my fantasy world, a similar legend exists—a godlike figure, Ondun, supposedly lives in an undiscovered kingdom far across this uncharted sea. The king of Tierra feels that if he just sends his ships sailing far off to the west to find this land, they can bring back such a powerful ally, and they can win victory over the Urabans once and for all.

But there's a catch: the Urabans have the same legend, and they believe if *they* can find Ondun, then he'll become *their* ally. So the king of Tierra sends his sailing ships westward across the uncharted Oceansea in search of Ondun … while the Sultan of Uraba sends *his* ships westward across the vast uncharted Middlesea. (And because the world is round, you can figure out what happens.…)

This grand quest leads to more important factors for the plot. In order to build those sailing ships, as well as to construct major navies to defend their lands, both Tierra and Uraba require a great deal of wood. Uraba (which is like Arabia) doesn't have a lot of forested land. [As a matter of historical fact, during the great boom of sailing ships and maritime trade, much of England's forests were denuded in order to construct enough ships.] Therefore, the Sultan of Uraba needs to expand into new territory where there is plentiful wood. Similarly, Uraba is poor in metals and mining, but Tierra has a rich set of mines on the northern coast of the Middlesea, the Gremurr Mines, a vulnerable place that the Urabans can attack. The mountains from the north block an easy retaliation from Tierra, unless a new road is scouted through the rugged territory....

You see how the landscape shapes the story?

Building this world, understanding and working with the geographical limitations, as well as where the resources were lacking, helped shaped the entire trilogy. I would call it more "inspirational   geography"   than   "wistful geography."

4.2
CLIMATE

Climate is more than just "It was a cloudy day outside." Climate drives an entire culture.

Think about it. A civilization that springs up on a lush tropical island, with plentiful water, fish, fruit, and moderate temperatures, will be very different from the culture that develops in an exceedingly harsh equatorial desert or in the frozen sub-arctic tundra.

Do your people live in a land with all the seasons, from hot summers to cold winters, or do they live in a temperate area where hunting, fishing, and agriculture continue throughout the year? When your survival depends on planting at a certain time, harvesting at a certain time, and preserving and storing lots of food for an entire season, your characters will have a different mindset than if they know every day is going to be basically the same.

Climate influences clothing styles and fabrics, and therefore *trade* in the materials to make those clothes. An extremely cold environment requires warm clothing, thick wool, or furs. The need for furs will make hunters go after game that they wouldn't necessarily eat, such as sables or minks (thick, warm fur, but not good to eat). In an extremely hot and humid climate, however, you won't see much demand for thick wool or warm furs. In a place like that, their clothing would be loose and cool, and traders would focus instead on fabrics like cotton and silk. The clothing styles may even be scanty or risqué, because the temperature outside is so darn hot. Or clothing is designed to keep away bugs, as in a mosquito-infested swamp.

Heavy heat and humidity can affect a culture in other ways. It's almost a cliché to describe the slow and lethargic daily life in the Deep South; the outside climate just saps the will to run around with great energy. On the other hand, you don't see too many sluggish, lethargic people lounging around in the bitter cold of a howling arctic storm.

Climate has an effect on food and cooking styles. In hot, moist climates where food spoils quickly, the locals tend to make heavily spiced dishes with hot peppers, which not only mask the taste of food starting to go bad, but also serve as a preservative, such as Indian food, Mexican food, or Thai food.

In colder climates where there is a seasonal component to hunting and fishing, the people have to gather and store a year's worth of food in a fairly short time period. They have been forced to discover many different ways of preserving perishables, such as drying, salting, pickling, even freezing. The next time you order ethnic food, think about some of the causes and connections. (such as, how did *deep-fried ice cream* become a traditional Mexican dish?)

Climate also affects language. Eskimo and Lapland tribes have dozens of words for different types of snow, while a native Saharan tribe wouldn't have much use for that vocabulary … although they probably have as many different descriptors for dunes and sand.

4.3
POLITICS

How does your society run?

Granted, it's been a long time since my high school civics class. When I watch the news, I couldn't entirely explain how our own government runs (if it actually does), but in a fictional world, you can lay out your own constitution or Magna Carta. Take over the land and run it from your authorial chair—how does it work?

Is your society a monarchy? If so, how does the succession run? First-born male child? First-born child of either sex? Is the throne run by women only, and the husbands are just figureheads? Does the leadership pass by right of mortal combat among all of the ruler's children, and may the best candidate win?

Is the ruler a usurper or tyrant, hated by all the downtrodden people while he struggles to consolidate a new reign? Or is it a rightful king or queen whose rule is not questioned?

Or is the land run by a council of elders? A council of nobles? If so, how are they chosen? Through inheritance, or merit, or randomly chosen by nametags drawn out of a cauldron? Are the council members honorable or corrupt?

During the Iraq War, some leaders believed (completely incorrectly, as it turns out) that the Iraqi people would happily cheer the American forces, view us as liberators, and celebrate our arrival, because "everyone wants democracy." But a democratic society requires certain cultural underpinnings and expectations from the people. Your characters would be in for a tremendous surprise if, for instance, they went back in time to 14th century France, killed off the monarchs, freed all the peasants and serfs, and said, "There, you're independent now! Form your own democracy." That might make for a very interesting novel, but not one, I suspect, that would have a happy ending.

Do your people live in a free culture where they are allowed to poke fun and make biting satirical commentary of the rulers, or are such comments swiftly and violently repressed?

Are the laws upheld or are they subject to bribery?

Is it a free-wheeling merchant state or a fascist dictatorship?

Even if the king, or council, or capital are far away and have little direct effect on your character's daily life, the government system still has an effect on your story. The society will change depending on whether the ruler is hated or beloved.

4.4
Economics

What do people do for a living? How do they pay their bills?

Unless your character is a trust fund baby, a filthy rich noble lord, or an alien species who can somehow gather nutrients by photosynthesizing from sunlight, he or she will want to know where their next meal is coming from. How will they acquire the necessities of getting from day to day? Where do they get shelter?

Any society has the basics of growing or acquiring food, and then distributing it (unless your character is only one person, getting food for herself), which leads to transportation needs and providers, merchants, as well as the subsidiary industries of cooks, restaurants, inns, and on and on. The same goes for resources: woodcutters, lumber mills, carpenters ... and miners, smelters, blacksmiths ... and quarry workers, stonecutters, masons. Everything *in* your society was created and built by someone.

In a high-tech science fiction society, such things are probably far removed from most of your characters (I don't think about where the plastic came from in the handle of my microwave oven when I push the buttons to heat up my cup of coffee), but if your society is much closer to subsistence level, those concerns really matter.

As a writer, if you have a character who is a farmer or a hunter, a fisherman, a caravan driver, a miner, you don't have to explain what they do or why when you build your world. But what if your economics are dependent on something more interesting? Is there some special commodity that's unique to the city or land—like the spice mélange in *Dune*, for example, a substance so rare and valuable that it is economically feasible for people to endure one of the most hellish environments in the Imperium just to obtain it. Or, closer to home, we have petroleum, some of the greatest reserves of which are buried under a harsh desert inhabited by often hostile people ... or found by drilling in the North Sea on oil rigs where the crews have to endure terrible storms and isolation.

What is valuable in your fictional society? If something is plentiful and easy to obtain, it's not likely to be very valuable. Is it a special kind of wood that grows in the dangerous rainforest? Is it a drug or medicine extracted from shellfish in a nearby shark-infested coral reef?

Or yak butter?

Let's explore yak butter for a minute. Imagine a kingdom where yak butter is a popular, and therefore valuable, commodity because King Thomas loves it. Thomas puts yak butter on his toast every morning, slathers yak butter on his sandwiches at lunch, and mixes great amounts of yak butter on his pasta at dinner. Because all the nobles at court want to earn favor with the king, they also use yak butter on almost everything.

This causes an economic boom for the yak herders in the isolated hill country. Never before has the demand for their yak butter been so high! Because of the higher profits and the higher demand, the wealthiest yak herders gather larger herds, and all that new money allows them to build bigger villages, have more children (because they can feed them now). They can even have more wives now (or husbands), if this is a society that allows it. Competing yak-butter merchants buy up the product as soon as it comes out of the churns, and they see that it gets distributed throughout the kingdom, particularly to the main castle. Caravans deliver the loads of yak butter, bringing it swiftly to market before it goes rancid, which leads to more heavily traveled roads through the mountains for efficient delivery.

It's a true boom time for the yak herders.

Unfortunately, after King Thomas dies mysteriously, his successor, King Ronald, hates yak butter. No, he *loathes* yak butter. He won't let his kitchens use it. He has all the supplies dumped in the moats and sweeps it out of the castle entirely. Therefore, all the fawning nobles at court suddenly discover that they, too, hate yak butter. Caravans are turned away. No one wants to buy the stuff throughout the kingdom. The yak herders in the hills are left high and dry, and they suffer a complete economic collapse.

But let's make it more interesting. Economics drive your *story* as well.

How about some characters—the main yak herder's daughter is in love with a boy who runs a caravan taking yak butter along the perilous mountain roads all the way to market in the capital city. He has many adventures delivering his cargo, while the daughter tends the herds and waits for her love to return.

But wait … what if it turns out that King Thomas was *poisoned* by a bad batch of yak butter … the very yak butter that the caravan boy just delivered? The boy is suddenly thrown under suspicion, but he escapes before King Ronald's guards can arrest him. The boy flees, running back to the shelter in the mountains to be reunited with his love, who of course believes he is innocent. King Ronald sends armies into the hills after the boy, and also to crush the yak herder settlements. He even outlaws yak butter because of the death of King Thomas … but of course *Ronald* is the one who slipped poison into the yak butter so that he can take the throne, and he's using the caravan boy and the scruffy yak herders as scapegoats. Why? Because one of his scouts has discovered a large gold vein in the mountains where the yak herders live, and he wants the territory for himself.…

You make up the rest.

4.5
SOCIETY

How are people treated in your fictional world? How do they get along every day? The social structure creates a framework for everything your characters do. A budding love story set in San Francisco during the Summer of Love will have a strikingly different feel than the same love story set in the Soviet Union under Stalin or in North Korea.

Are people happy and pursuing dreams in their everyday life, or do they live in a repressive world, tight-lipped and fearful at any moment?

Is your population treated equally, or is there a rigid class system? If there is general equality among the sexes and races (and species, in certain science fiction or fantasy titles), then your character interactions can proceed however you like. A strict class system, however, adds an entirely different framework.

How do people interact inside and outside of their rigidly defined classes? Are there extremely differentiated castes, or just a general spectrum from the powerful to the powerless? The wealthy and the poor? They will *act* differently to one another.

Once, when I was staying in a hotel, the housekeeper had done a particularly good job (straightened my clothes, left extra towels, added a few extra touches), and I saw on the hotel's notecard that my room had been serviced by "Desiree." As I went to get my morning coffee, I walked past the supply room to find some of the housekeepers, chatting, working, laughing, telling jokes, generally enjoying themselves. When I returned, I passed one of the young women moving her cart along the corridor, and when I saw that her name tag said Desiree, I stopped. "Are you Desiree? Thanks for doing a very nice job with my room." This was one of the staff who had been casually chatting and laughing with her coworkers only a few minutes earlier. I wasn't expecting anything more than a smile and "Thanks. Enjoy your stay." But as soon as I spoke with her, she instantly averted her eyes, took a step aside so I could easily get past her in the hall, and mumbled nervously, "Thank you, sir." I found it very strange.

If your story operates with a system of nobility, how do the lessers address the people from above their station? Growing up in the U.S., I've never truly fathomed the labyrinth of titles—Sir, My Lord, Your Grace, My Liege, Eminence, and You Idiot—though I suspect it has something to do with the equally convoluted menagerie of counts, dukes, barons, viscounts, princes, grand dukes, and the like.

Are there slaves, and if so how are they treated? Are they miserable, whipped, overworked, and tortured ... or are they an accepted part of society and treated reasonably well? Prisoners of war and their descendants, for example.

What about serfs and peasants, the workers of the land? Serfs are often forced into their servitude by a great debt that they owe and can never repay, nor can their descendants. What are the mechanics for how your slaves or serfs can be freed? This would certainly give a character a great deal of hope and a goal. And is it a real chance—or just a scam?

How are women treated? Are they considered objects of great beauty? Held inside a noble house and never let outside? Or forced to cover up every part of their skin so that no other men can be jealous? Are they kept barefoot and pregnant, or are they equal partners in society? Are they allowed to be educated? Are they revered and worshipped as in a great matriarchy?

Do your people have large families, celebrating as many children as possible? Or are they limited (perhaps by the government) to one or possibly two offspring?

How are children treated? Are they forced into rigid behavior, never allowed to be rambunctious, "seen and not heard," or are they allowed to run wild, like lost boys and girls, not given any responsibilities or behavior controls until they reach near adulthood?

How does your society treat the sick and poor? Are there beggars in the streets, or can anyone find a job to earn room and board when needed? Are the sick cared for with benevolent healers, or are they abandoned, left to die? "to decrease the surplus population," as Ebenezer Scrooge would have it.

What about the elderly? Are they revered or considered a burden and a waste of resources? When a wise old person grows shaky and infirm, is he appreciated for all his life experience and wisdom, or is he cast out from the tribe and sent into the cold to starve and die?

You will have population centers. Are the cities sprawling, open, and welcoming ... or do the people huddle behind high city walls? Do they live in enclosed habitat domes, or in a vast open landscape where the nearest neighbor is hours away?

How does communication work in your society, particularly long-distance communication? How is news spread? How do people know about the rest of the world? Do they use carrier pigeons? Runners and rumor-spreaders? Are there magic scrying mirrors or contract telepaths? Does your society have the printing press for preservation and dissemination of information, or are squinty-eyed monks in dim rooms busily copying tomes as best they can?

How does the military fit into society? Does the ruler hire mercenary forces or security troops when she feels the need? Is there a large standing army (which requires a significant expense and therefore higher taxes—see *Economics* above)? Is it a volunteer army, or is conscription enforced? Does every young man, or young woman, know they will have to serve in the army? Does the army use horses or ground vehicles? Do they fight with swords? Gunpowder and firearms? Magic spells, telepathic blasts, bolts of lightning summoned from the clouds?

On the flip side of warfare and defense, what do the people do for *fun*? What are the main leisure activities? Do they let mad bulls chase them through the streets and call it fun? (No, nobody would believe that!) Are there particularly interesting sports, perhaps some that require individual exercise and physical prowess, or others that have become team sports? And in team competitions, what do the winners receive—a trophy? A large monetary reward? A free annual pass to the local brothel? And what happens to the losers? Do they go home in shame to practice for next year? Do they have their heads chopped off, as in ancient Mayan ball games? Are the players gladiators, whose very life depends on winning every match?

What about games? Nearly every society has some form of gambling for amusement. Is the gambling open or illicit?

And what about drugs? Are they commonplace and socially accepted for the most part, like caffeine, alcohol, or tobacco … or are they potent and illegal? What are the penalties for use? What are the addictions, and the consequences?

(PAUSE)
TAKE A BREATH

Let me pause here to let you catch your breath, and for me to give you a reality check:

You don't have to answer every one of these questions for the world you're creating—but at least think about them, especially the ones that have something to do with your specific story and characters.

When you start turning over the creative rocks and looking at what might scurry out, the very answers you concoct might spark story ideas or new characters, or just interesting background details that will make your world stand out.

Now you have an idea why so many of my books turn into massive tomes!

4.6
RELIGION

Religion (or rival religions) is one of the primary drivers in a world, shaping many aspects of culture and society. Unless your world is basically secular, with the people primarily concerned about politics and commerce, religion will form a strong set of guardrails on your plotline. Are they spiked iron guardrails, or cushy velvet-covered ones?

What sort of god or gods do the people worship? Are they benevolent, nurturing paternal or maternal figures, or are they scary monsters that demand sacrifices? Or are the "gods" mere philosophical concepts for comfort and enlightenment, like an esoteric Higher Power.

In some societies, the people have an up-close and personal *real* interaction with their god(s)—for instance, if your ruler is a godlike priest-king or if, as in Greek mythology, the pantheon of gods actually does come down to interact regularly and personally with everyday people (usually meddling, testing, or getting some poor girl pregnant).

If the gods themselves don't have an actual walk-on role in your story, the organized religion may be powerful enough to dominate much of the activity. If you set your story in Saudi Arabia, think of how much Islam shapes every aspect of daily life. A blonde single mother searching for love in Afghanistan would be an entirely different story from a romance with the same character in Paris. If your character breaks a religious law, is he frowned upon by a prune-faced church lady, or does he have his hands chopped off?

Is your religion powerful and monolithic, like the Catholic Church in Europe in the Middle Ages? Or are there various churches, sects, cults, and traditions? If so, how are the others tolerated? Is there a grab-bag of cults all vying for new members, or are any new religions forced to meet in secret back rooms? If your character lives in a village controlled by ISIS, he's not likely to attend public debates on comparative religions. On the other hand, Islam in the Middle Ages tended to be much more open and pragmatic. Although Islam was the official religion, Christians and Jews were tolerated, so long as they paid an extra tax.

What about the priests and the priesthood? Are they respected? Are they allowed to marry and have children? Are they literate? (Are they perhaps the *only* literate people in a peasant-based society?)

Note also that a formal organized church is often the basis of a codified system of laws and criminal punishment ... and that certainly has a bearing on what will actually happen when the poor yak butter caravan boy is arrested on suspicion of poisoning the king....

Even in a relatively open culture, religious aspects can permeate other activities (this overlaps with *Society*, above). Just try to order a normal alcoholic drink in a restaurant in southern Utah, and you'll immediately see the Mormon influence in everyday non-church life. Once, while staying in Monticello, Utah, I asked the front desk clerk where I might buy a six-pack of beer for the refrigerator in my room. He responded with a horrified expression, as if I had tried to score heroin. "Oh, no, sir! We don't carry any of that here in this town! You have to go fifty miles away to find a liquor store." Even then, fifty miles away, the option was a blocky prison-like building on a side street called a "State-Run Liquor Store," where they sold only warm beer, nothing refrigerated. When I asked if they had any cold beer, I was again greeted with similar horror. "Oh no, sir! We can't sell *cold* beer, because then you might go home and drink it right away."

No, I couldn't make that up. Imagine the shock a complete outsider would have entering a situation like that.

Similarly, the Southern Baptist Church has made the state of Texas a patchwork of contradictions, a state full of fiercely independent people who vigorously fight against any limits on their freedoms ... yet they also have seven completely dry counties where no sales of alcohol of any kind are allowed; sometimes these counties are adjacent to other completely "wet" counties featuring drive-up liquor stores where a person can pull up to the window and a helpful clerk will pop open a can of beer and hand it to you before you drive off.

When you create your fictional world, though, I suggest you have it make more sense than the real world.

4.7
INTELLECTUAL /
SCIENCE

This subject goes hand-in-hand with *Religion* (or sometimes hand-in-fist), heart vs. mind, rational vs. faith.

How do people think the world works? When your characters hear thunder in the sky, do they believe gods are battling in the clouds, or do they know it's hot and cold air masses colliding in the atmosphere? Do they know where the sun goes at night?

How advanced is their astronomy? Developing a basic calendar is more important than just remembering your significant other's birthday or anniversary. In an agricultural society, knowing the turn of the seasons, when floods might come, when to plant and when to harvest, can be the difference between survival and extinction.

Does everyone have a basic scientific understanding, or are scientists—alchemists, astronomers—revered and mysterious, like high priests or magicians?

Are scientists revered or feared? Think of the Professor on *Gilligan's Island*, who was basically an all-knowing wizard who could come up with the solution to any problem, related to any conceivable scientific discipline (usually using vines and coconuts as his raw materials). Or Willow on *Buffy the Vampire Slayer* who could look up the vital piece of information to be used against any monster from her mountain of ancient books (all this, obviously, before the advent of Google searches).

Again, tied in with the section on **Society**, how widespread is education? Is it open and available to everyone, or just to an elite? Let's get even more basic—does everyone know how to read and write? Do they understand mathematics? Or is such knowledge limited to a secret cabal of experts?

How much does the government control the education system? Does the queen want all of her subjects to have a full education, to understand the basic geography of the world and to learn other languages? Or does the ruling council control the population through selective and cultivated ignorance?

What is the state of medicine, and hence, what is the state of biological knowledge? Are there large hospitals and medical schools with dissection laboratories, or are there just local healers using traditional remedies and "old wives tale" knowledge passed from generation to generation?

Are women allowed to be educated? And if so, are there specific professions in which they specialize? Can they be doctors or just midwives? Does the local healer who knows an herbal remedy for any ailment, practice with impunity … or is she considered an eccentric oddball in danger of being stoned as a witch?

Are philosophers allowed to ruminate on the nature of existence, to question the foundations of society and politics, on morality, on commonly held religious beliefs, or are they burned at the stake for speaking blasphemy? If they question the natural order, do they have to do it in whispers among like-minded students?

And, as mentioned earlier, how is information disseminated? Is there the printing press? Are books widely available in free libraries to anyone who wants to read them (again, assuming they can all read)? Or do secret societies keep treasure troves of repressed information? Are there elaborate scientific societies and universities, or just crackpot inventors working in a shed behind the garage?

Does your scientist character have the power to save the world or destroy it ... or maybe he could just develop a chemical means to detect poison in tainted yak butter.

4.8
ARTS

Artistic expression is what gives a society its "look and feel."

Let's start with architecture as the most obvious example. When your character arrives in a new city or a foreign land, what does she see? Think of the graceful domes and minaret spires if the city is Istanbul or an Arabian nights Baghdad ... or the cold and blocky buildings of Soviet-era Warsaw. (Yes, I have been to both.) Think of the soaring stone castles and cathedrals in Europe, the wooden churches of Scandinavia, the low adobe pueblos of the American Southwest.

Architecture and the design is usually driven by the climate and the raw materials available. (Again, refer to various sections above—see, I told you it was all connected.)

Are the city buildings painted with bright beautiful frescoes, or brilliant primary colors, or are they subdued—grays, whites, tans? Are the buildings themselves considered beautiful, or just utilitarian? Is your city cluttered with statues, fountains and monuments everywhere? And if so, are they genuine works of art— maybe free-form designs, or sculptures of great legendary heroes—or are they erected for propaganda purposes, fifty idealized statues of the current repressive leader?

Is there a specific style of music? Do the minstrels play folk songs, or impassioned religious hymns, or do they sing thinly disguised commentary on current events? Do they play interesting musical instruments—flutes, drums, stringed instruments? Accordions? The yak herders might be well known for their sweet accordion music. Maybe our caravan boy plays the accordion to himself on the long journey to trade his yak butter, as he misses his sweetheart.

Note that each of those instruments is small enough and portable enough that a wandering minstrel can carry one. (You don't see many traveling minstrels hauling a piano around with them.)

Art—decorations, paintings, sculptures, music, writing, and poetry—is an indicator of the extent of free expression. Are people allowed to be imaginative and even eccentric in creating new works? That sort of thing happens only in a free *and prosperous* society. In a squalid subsistence-farming village or in a nomadic tribe in the drought-stricken Serengeti, you won't find many people supporting themselves full-time through poetry (although even harsh societies tend to value minstrels and storytellers). Of course, I should point out that there aren't many full-time poets who can support themselves even in the modern western world.

Do painters take commissions or simply try to sell their works in the bazaar? Is there a printing press to reproduce the poems or stories so that a writer's work can be printed and distributed, or are the tales simply passed along orally, as Homer did?

And, back to *Economics*, how does the artist survive in your society? Do minstrels sing for their supper? Do painters and writers have wealthy patrons who support them? Or are they like modern-day writers, writing and writing and writing, submitting and submitting and submitting, all in hopes of earning just a few cents a word?

4.9
HISTORY

Your world has a history, and even if the characters don't know all the names and dates, they will have a general awareness of where they come from and what happened before.

When writing an epic, authors often develop the full and elaborate history of their world as background work. And after putting so much work into all that history, obviously they want to use it. All of it. But remember, no one knows all the details. It doesn't matter what the author has written down, if the character doesn't know the information, don't include it.

What happened before your story starts? Has there been a long-standing peace, and your people are relaxed and confident of where they'll be in a year or a decade, or have the characters lived through an endless succession of political upheavals and the resulting social turmoil? Is the land in the midst of a revolution (for good or bad), or is it relatively stagnant?

Is your story set in a newly formed colony where settlers are scraping out a living and starting everything from scratch? Or do they live in an ancient city steeped in centuries of history and traditions?

Were your people recently conquered and now live under disliked overlords, or are they the conquerors themselves, trying to quell any dissatisfaction among the new subjects? Remember, winners and losers will have an entirely different version of what happened— even about recent events, as well as long-standing historical occurrences.

Most people will only know the history that's relevant to them. Don't expect a peasant to be able to rattle off the entire succession of monarchs and the dates of their reigns. They will likely know who the current ruler is, and possibly the previous one, and maybe a particularly famous, revered, or hated one from the past.

Quick, off the top of your head—what was the greatest foreign-policy achievement of President Millard Fillmore? That's not something likely to come up in general conversation. (I actually happen to know the answer—Fillmore was the president who opened trade with isolationist Japan to the west.)

The knowledge of major historical characters—heroes, villains, saints—was often passed along in oral legends, folklore, and songs. Most of you won't know much about Duke Wenceslaus I who ruled Bohemia in the 10th Century, but you've probably heard the popular Christmas carol "Good King Wenceslas."

In his epic "Song of Ice and Fire," George R.R. Martin developed an immense history of rulers and dynasties, generations of characters, countless intricate betrayals and assassinations. Many of those details are genuinely relevant to the characters who are members of the noble families torn apart. If your family lost its prominence and went bankrupt because of the murder of a king, you would certainly know the details of that event, even if it happened generations ago, because families tend to hold grudges. Even if your character is a commoner, she might know some of that political history because of all the turmoil the entire land went through in the resulting civil wars and struggles.

But she won't know *all* the details, and what she does know might not be accurate.

Let me emphasize—no matter how much meticulous detail you put into developing the entire history of your world

DON'T INCLUDE EVERYTHING!

Historical details are like seasoning thrown in to enhance, but not overwhelm, the flavor of your story.

4.10
REVIEWING THE INGREDIENTS

Now, let's review and put the pieces together as to how they can be applied to your writing, how the ingredients are relevant to the story you want to tell.

GCPESRIAH

Geography—My small town of Franksville was in rural Wisconsin, with rolling hills and lots of fertile farmland that made it particularly suited to growing cabbage.

Climate—Even though the sauerkraut factory kept producing all year long, the fermented cabbage juice in the drainage ditches would freeze solid in the cold Wisconsin winter, so that my mother could go ice-skating on the kraut pond. Then, in spring, all that juice would thaw, and then rot, filling the air with an amazing stench.

Politics—As a kid in a small town, the actual local politics weren't relevant to me, though I know there was a mayor, a town council, the power brokers who ran the annual Kraut Festival, even the Rotary Club (where much of the town's business was conducted).

Economics—The sauerkraut factory was the main industry and driving economic factor in Franksville, and sauerkraut influenced so many aspects of the area, from the crops the cabbage farmers grew, to what the truckers hauled, to the workers in the kraut factory, to the administrators of the Kraut Festival, even my father, who ran the small town bank.

Society—Franksville was a very traditional Midwestern small town with yellow school buses, red barns, 1960s-era housewives who sat around the kitchen every morning smoking cigarettes and chatting in their coffee klatsches, while their husbands went off to work. Most of my neighbors were my cousins. Everybody knew everybody, and no one locked their doors.

Religion—The only church in Franksville was the Methodist Church, with white siding, a tall steeple, and black shingled roof. When my grandmother, a staunch Sicilian Catholic, moved to town with my grandfather, she had hoped to raise her five children in the Catholic Church, but had to settle for having them attend the Methodist church, because, she said, it was better than nothing.

Intellectual/Science—I was the smart kid with thick glasses and a fascination with comic books and science fiction. I always made the honor roll, often got straight A's. Although my parents were very pleased with this, I was mercilessly harassed by classmates who reviled me for being a "brain," gave me wedgies, and called me names so that I was forced to pretend not to be as smart as I really was.

Arts—I wanted to be a writer from the time I was five years old. I wanted to read books, but we had no public library, and I had to rely on the infrequent (and poorly stocked) Book-

Mobile. My parents purchased a library of paperback classics, which we kept at home, and I diligently worked my way through them.

History—My great grandparents, Andrew and Elsie Anderson, had come off the boat from Denmark and settled in southern Wisconsin. Their son, my grandfather, Jens Thornvig Anderson, kept up the family farm and became a pig farmer during World War II; he was not allowed to go over and fight, because farmers were considered vital to the war effort. My grandpa became the caretaker of the nearby county park, the place where the Kraut Festival was held each year.

My dad and his brother and sisters grew up in Franksville, and when they got old enough and married, they build houses on plots of land carved out from the acreage my grandpa had used in the original farm. As a high school student, my dad started work as a bookkeeper for the local fuel-oil company, and was good enough at it that he started to work for the Bank of Franksville.

(All of these details were irrelevant to my daily life, but in developing the background world, it helps to know them.)

●   ●   ●

There, you see that even painting a picture of a perfectly common small American town requires from the same worldbuilding techniques as an entire fictional universe.

CONCLUSION
IS YOUR WORLD
FINISHED?

I hope I've given you a lot to think about in this book, a pile of kindling to start your imagination on fire.

Most users of a How-To book come looking for answers, and I'm afraid I've provided mostly pages and pages of questions. But that's the point: questions. You have to ask the questions, a lot of them, because the answers you come up with will form the very foundation of the world in which your story is set.

Let me reiterate my admonition from the previous section, though: **DON'T INCLUDE EVERYTHING**.

Just because I've listed a hundred questions, your story doesn't require answers for all of them. You don't need to know every single thing, if it doesn't affect your story—and the reader certainly doesn't know (and it probably isn't interested in), every last detail from the beginning of the world.

Asking those questions, though, is like adding creative fertilizer. When you work with all those ingredients and build your world, your story and characters will naturally blossom from it.

ABOUT THE AUTHOR

Kevin J. Anderson is the author of 130 novels, more than fifty of which have appeared on national or international bestseller lists; he has over 23 million books in print in thirty languages. He has won or been nominated for the Hugo Award, Nebula Award, Bram Stoker Award, Shamus Award, the SFX Reader's Choice Award, and New York Times Notable Book.

Anderson has coauthored fourteen books in the Dune saga with Brian Herbert. Anderson's popular epic SF series, The Saga of Seven Suns, is his most ambitious work, as well as its sequel, The Saga of Shadows. He has also written a sweeping fantasy trilogy, Terra Incognita, accompanied by two rock CDs based on the novels (which he wrote and produced). He has written two steampunk fantasy adventure novels, *Clockwork Angels* and *Clockwork Lives*, with legendary Rush drummer and lyricist Neil Peart. He also created the popular humorous horror series featuring Dan Shamble, Zombie PI.

His novel *Enemies & Allies* chronicles the first meeting of Batman and Superman in the 1950s; Anderson also wrote *The Last Days of Krypton*. He has written numerous Star Wars projects, including the Jedi Academy trilogy, the Young Jedi Knights series (with Moesta), and Tales of the Jedi comics from Dark Horse. Fans might also know him from his X-Files novels or Dean Koontz's *Frankenstein: Prodigal Son*.

IF YOU LIKED ...

If you liked *Worldbuilding,* you might also enjoy:

Million Dollar Productivity
Kevin J. Anderson

Million Dollar Professionalism
Kevin J. Anderson & Rebecca Moesta

Million Dollar Outlines
David Farland

Clockwork Angels: The Comic Book Scripts
Kevin J. Anderson & Neil Peart

OTHER
WORDFIRE
PRESS TITLES

Our list of other WordFire Press authors and titles is always
growing. To find out more and to see our selection of titles,
visit us at:

wordfirepress.com